PERSONNEL ADMINISTRATION SCHOOL
MARINE CORPS COMBAT SERVICE SUPPORT SCHOOLS

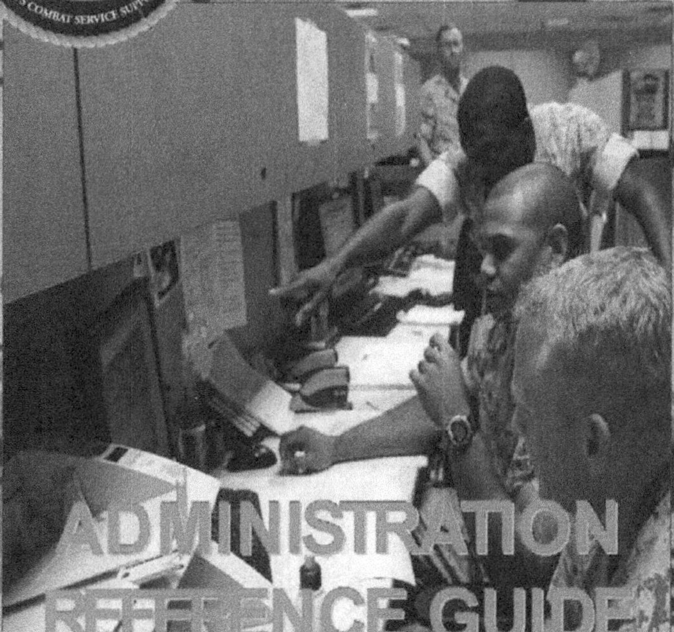

ADMINISTRATION REFERENCE GUIDE

DISTRIBUTION STATEMENT A: Approved for public release, distribution is unlimited

PCN: 50100121200

Administration Reference Guide
Table of Contents

Leadership is the sum of those qualities of intellect, human understanding, and moral character that enables a person to inspire and to control a group of people successfully.

Marine Corps Leadership Principles
1. Be technically and tactically proficient.
2. Know yourself and seek self-improvement.
3. Know your Marines and look out for their welfare.
4. Keep your Marines informed.
5. Set the example.
6. Ensure that the task is understood, supervised and accomplished.
7. Train your Marines as a team.
8. Make sound and timely decisions.
9. Develop a sense of responsibility among subordinates.
10. Employ your Marines in accordance with their capabilities.
11. Seek responsibility and take responsibility for your actions.

Marine Corps Leadership Traits

Judgment – The quality of weighing facts and possible solutions on which to base sound decisions.

Justice – The quality of being impartial and consistent in exercising command.

Decisiveness – Ability to reach decisions promptly and to announce them in a clear, forceful manner.

Initiative – Seeing what has to be done and commencing a course of action, even in the absence of orders.

Dependability – The certainty of the proper performance of duty.

Tact – The ability to deal with others without creating offense.

Integrity – Uprightness of character and soundness of moral principle, absolute truthfulness and honesty.

Enthusiasm – The display of sincere interest and exuberance in the performance of duty.

Bearing – Creating a favorable impression in carriage, appearance, and personal conduct at all times.

Unselfishness – Avoidance of providing for ones comfort and personal advancement at the expense of others.

Courage – A mental quality that recognizes fear of danger or criticism but enables a Marine to proceed in the face of it with calmness and firmness.

Knowledge – Acquired information, including professional knowledge and an understanding of your Marines.

Loyalty – Faithfulness to God, country, Corps, unit, and to your seniors and subordinates.

Endurance – The mental and physical stamina measured by the ability to withstand pain, fatigue, distress and hardship.

Objectives of Leadership
Primary – Accomplishment of mission.
Secondary – Welfare of the Marines.

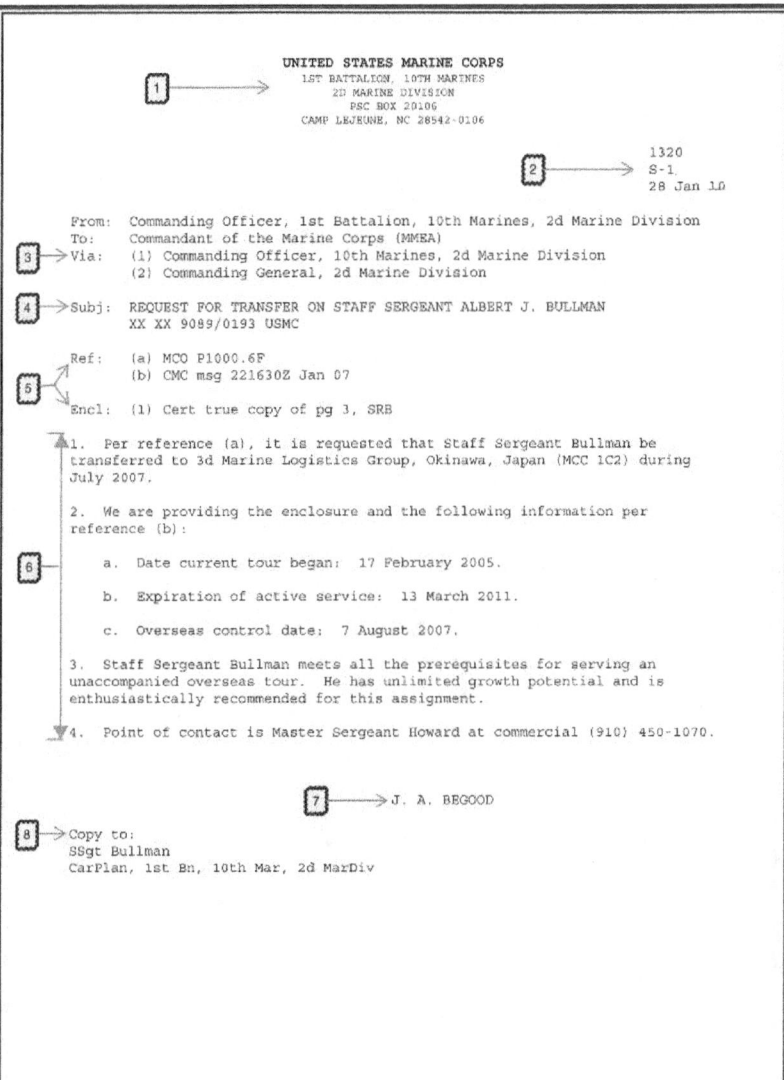

UNITED STATES MARINE CORPS
1ST BATTALION, 10TH MARINES
2D MARINE DIVISION
PSC BOX 20106
CAMP LEJEUNE, NC 28542-0106

1320
S-1
28 Jan 10

From: Commanding Officer, 1st Battalion, 10th Marines, 2d Marine Division
To: Commandant of the Marine Corps (MMEA)
Via: (1) Commanding Officer, 10th Marines, 2d Marine Division
     (2) Commanding General, 2d Marine Division

Subj: REQUEST FOR TRANSFER ON STAFF SERGEANT ALBERT J. BULLMAN
XX XX 9089/0193 USMC

Ref: (a) MCO P1000.6F
     (b) CMC msg 221630Z Jan 07

Encl: (1) Cert true copy of pg 3, SRB

1. Per reference (a), it is requested that Staff Sergeant Bullman be transferred to 3d Marine Logistics Group, Okinawa, Japan (MCC 1C2) during July 2007.

2. We are providing the enclosure and the following information per reference (b):

   a. Date current tour began: 17 February 2005.

   b. Expiration of active service: 13 March 2011.

   c. Overseas control date: 7 August 2007.

3. Staff Sergeant Bullman meets all the prerequisites for serving an unaccompanied overseas tour. He has unlimited growth potential and is enthusiastically recommended for this assignment.

4. Point of contact is Master Sergeant Howard at commercial (910) 450-1070.

                                        J. A. BEGOOD

Copy to:
SSgt Bullman
CarPlan, 1st Bn, 10th Mar, 2d MarDiv

Standard Letter Guidelines

1 - **Letterhead** - Top line is typed in Courier New, 10 pitch, and in bold. Rest of letterhead is typed in Courier New, 8 pitch. Page 11 of SECNAVINST 5216.5D.

2 - **Identification Symbols** - Consists of SSIC, office code, and date in the abbreviated format shown on the standard letter example. Page 33 of SECNAVINST 5216.5D.

3 - **Via** - Use when one or more activities outside of your own should see the letter before it reaches the "To:" address. Do not number if there is only one via. Page 38 of SECNAVINST 5216.5D.

4 - **Subject Line** - All caps, no abbreviations. Page 38 of SECNAVINST 5216.5D.

5 - **Reference/Enclosure** - Indicate references with a letter and enclosures with a number, even if there is only one. Ensure all references and enclosures are identified in the text, in the order they are listed. Page 38 - 42 of SECNAVINST 5216.5D.

6 - **Text/Paragraphs** - A signature page must have at least two lines of text, do not use abbreviations, and utilize the 4-8-12 indentation rule which can be found on page 56 of SECNAVINST 5216.5D.

7 - **Signature Block** - First initial starts at the center of the page. Do not center the whole name. Last name is in caps, unless the last name starts with a prefix. Page 44 of SECNAVINST 5216.5D.

8 - **Copy To Block** - Maximum abbreviation. Does not have to be in order of seniority, use this block for individuals or units that need to know the letter's content but don't need to act on it. Page 45 of SECNAVINST 5216.5D.

Information for second and succeeding pages of a standard letter

* - Subject line is always typed on the second and all succeeding pages.

* - Start typing on the sixth line.

* - There is no need for letterhead since it is already identified on the first page.

* - Always put a page number on the second and succeeding pages. Page number will be centered and one half inch from the bottom.

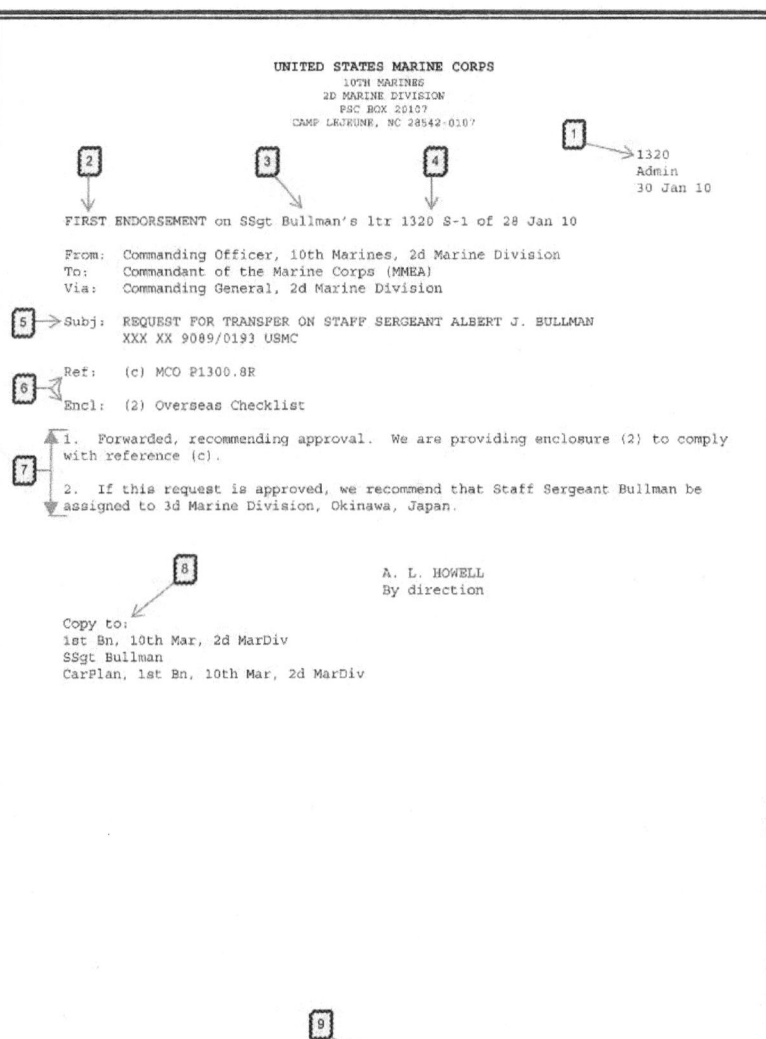

UNITED STATES MARINE CORPS
10TH MARINES
2D MARINE DIVISION
PSC BOX 20107
CAMP LEJEUNE, NC 28542-0107

1320
Admin
30 Jan 10

FIRST ENDORSEMENT on SSgt Bullman's ltr 1320 S-1 of 28 Jan 10

From: Commanding Officer, 10th Marines, 2d Marine Division
To: Commandant of the Marine Corps (MMEA)
Via: Commanding General, 2d Marine Division

Subj: REQUEST FOR TRANSFER ON STAFF SERGEANT ALBERT J. BULLMAN
        XXX XX 9089/0193 USMC

Ref: (c) MCO P1300.8R

Encl: (2) Overseas Checklist

1. Forwarded, recommending approval. We are providing enclosure (2) to comply
with reference (c).

2. If this request is approved, we recommend that Staff Sergeant Bullman be
assigned to 3d Marine Division, Okinawa, Japan.

                                        A. L. HOWELL
                                        By direction

Copy to:
1st Bn, 10th Mar, 2d MarDiv
SSgt Bullman
CarPlan, 1st Bn, 10th Mar, 2d MarDiv

2

3

New Page Endorsement Guidelines

1 - **Identification Symbols** - SSIC will always repeat the basic document's SSIC.

2 - **Endorsement Line** - Type number of endorsement in all caps. First via addressess would be "FIRST ENDORSEMENT," second via would be "SECOND ENDORSEMENT."

3 - **Endorsement Line** - The "From" line of the original letter/AA Form.

4 - **Endorsement Line** - Information comes from the standard letter or the AA Form identification symbols block of the original document.

5 - **Subject Line** - The subject line will stay the same as the original document. Do not modify or change.

6 - **References/Enclosures** - Do not repeat references/enclosures already mentioned in the original document. If adding a reference/enclosure, ensure they are properly annotated in sequence to the original document. Must be mentioned in the text, in order.

7 - **Text/Paragraphs** - Endorsements are utilized to forward comments, make recommendations, and provide information. Remarks should be short and to the point. If large amounts of information or documentation needs to be added it should be typed separately and included as an enclosure.

8 - **Copy To Block** - All previous recipients should receive a copy as well as the originator of the original document and previous endorsements.

9 - **Page Numbering** - Page numbering continues the same as the standard letter. If the original standard letter has one page then the first endorsement will be page 2.

Same-Page Endorsement Guidelines

* - Same-page endorsements may omit the SSIC and subject line. The basic letters identification can also be removed from the endorsement line.

Example and more information for a same page endorsement can be found on page 68 of SECNAVINST 5216.5D

ADMINISTRATIVE ACTION (5216) NAVMC 10274 (REV. 3-93) (EF) Previous editions will be used SN: 0109-LF-063-3200 U/I: PADS OF 100		1. ACTION NO. S-1	2. SSIC/FILE NO. 1336
		3. DATE 15 Jan 10	

4. FROM (Grade, Name, SSN, MOS, or CO, Pers. O., etc.)	5. ORGANIZATION AND STATION (Complete address)
Cpl Kevin D. Wagner XXX XX 9021/0331 USMC Abbreviation optional	COA, 1st Bn 10th Mar, 2d MarDiv PSC Box 20106 CamLej 28542-0106 Abbreviation optional
6. VIA (As required) (1) CO COA, 1stBn 10thMar 2dMarDiv (2) CO 1stBn 10thMar 2d MarDiv (3) CO 10thMar (4) CG 2dMarDiv	

7. TO:	Commandant of the Marine Corps (MMEA-85) Headquarters US Mairne Corps Quantico, VA 22134-0004	8. NATURE OF ACTION/SUBJECT RE FOR PCSO TO MARINE SECURITY GUARD SCOL Abbreviation optional
		9. COPY TO (As required) SgtMaj, MCB, CamLej

10. REFERENCE OR AUTHORITY (if applicable) (a) MCO P1000.6G (b) MCO P1326.6D or None or N/A	11. ENCLOSURES (if any) (1) Cert true copy of BIR/BTR (2) Commanding Officer's Screening/Interview Guide or None or N/A

12. SUPPLEMENTAL INFORMATION (Reduce to minimum wording - type name of orginator and sign 3 lines below text)

1. Per ref (a), I re PCSO to Marine Security Guard scol, QUANT (MCC R00) dur Jun 10.

2. In add to encl (1), the fol info is provided:

   a. DCTB: 3 May 08.

   b. ECC: 13 Sep 12.

   c. Marital status: divorced.

3. Encl (2) is sub per ref (b).

4. I am willing to ext or reenl to have suf OBLSVC to accept this requested asg.

K. D. WAGNER

Abbreviation are used in this block

13. PROCESSING ACTION. (Complete processing action in item 12 or on reverse. Endorse by rubber stamp where practicable.)

Designed using FormFlow 2.15, HQMC/ARAE May 98

MCO 5216.19 contains step by step instructions on how
to fill out the AA Form

5

UNITED STATES MARINE CORPS
1ST BATTALION, 6TH MARINES
2D MARINE DIVISION
PSC BOX 1775
CAMP LEJEUNE, NC 28542

19 Jan 10

INFORMATION PAPER

Subj: INFORMATION PAPER FORMAT

Purpose: Present information in a summarized format.

Key Points: Following points pertain to information paper format.

-Use bullets when writing each point

-Present facts

-Address issues/concerns

-Specify objectives

-Commonly used acronyms/abbreviations are acceptable

-Acronyms such as BAMCIS, SMEAC, MEP

-Abbreviations such as LtCol, MarDiv, encl

Recommendation: If required.

Prepared by: GySgt Faval Datsuk, S-1, 450-9110

Classified by: _____
Declassify on: _____

Information Paper Guidelines

- Normally used to provide facts in a clear and concise format.

- Commonly used to prepare recipient for meetings, briefings, and discussions.

- Should be self-explanatory and require no enclosures, endorsements or attachments.

- Letterhead format is not required, but can be utilized.

- General format is not as important as accuracy of content.

- One page is preferred, two pages maximum.

- Tailor the paper to fit the need.

- Use standard bullets as provided by Microsoft Word, or word processing program.

- If document is classified, refer to MCO P5510.18, unit S-2 or Classified Material Control Center for proper marking and storage requirements.

UNITED STATES MARINE CORPS
1ST BATTALION, 6TH MARINES
2D MARINE DIVISION
PSC BOX 1775
CAMP LEJEUNE, NC 28542

20 Mar 10

POINT PAPER

Subj: POINT PAPER FORMAT

BACKGROUND: Why you are writing, sets context for discussion introduction of points, history of subject matter.

1. Word points are written as short, concise statements.

2. The keys to short, concise statements are:

    a. Brevity.

    b. Clarity.

3. Arrange points in logical or chronological sequence.

4. Include preparer or presenter information, including name, rank, office/section and telephone number.

5. If paper is unclassified, leave off classification markings and the classify/declassify lines.

6. Commonly accepted abbreviations and acronyms (GySgt, BAMCIS) are acceptable and encouraged.

SUMMARY: Summarize the key points. Indicate any position or conclusion that is appropriate or required.

Eric Staal, Capt, G-3 Ops, 450-1775

Classified by: _____
Declassify on: _____

Point Paper Guidelines

- Begin with background paragraph.

- Presents key points, facts, positions or questions in brief, orderly fashion.

- Sometimes referred to as discussion paper.

- Normally used as a reminder, assumes that reader has complete knowledge of subject.

- Logical sequence desired, but not mandatory.

- Should not exceed one page.

- Attachments or enclosures are authorized if required.

- Tables, graphs and charts can be incorporated or attached.

- Summary paragraph is required.

- Include preparer/point of contact information.

- If document is classified, refer to MCO P5510.18, unit S-2 or Classified Material Control Center for proper marking and storage requirements.

UNITED STATES MARINE CORPS
1ST BATTALION, 6TH MARINES
2D MARINE DIVISION
PSC BOX 1775
CAMP LEJEUNE, NC 28542

1 Apr 10

POSITION PAPER

Subj: FORMAT OF A POSITION PAPER

Ref: (a) MCO P1020.17

1. Purpose: To whom, and for what reasons are the questions to answer in this paragraph.

2. Requirement: Briefly state why a position is required. Include whether or not it is directed by higher headquarters.

3. Background/Discussion

a. Tailor discussion to the needs and knowledge of the reader. Subparagraphs such as Participants, Issues, Facts, Views, Opposing Views, Staff Position, Fallback Position or Conclusion may be used.

b. Write in a short, direct, conversational style that allows the reader to understand the key points and come to a logical conclusion. Avoid jargon, use active voice.

c. Put in concise terms the position to be discussed, or background of position.

d. Provide answers to potential questions.

e. Point should stand alone and not require amplification by subordinate points.

4. Position of other agencies/units: If appropriate, indicate position of other units. If there is none, indicate "Not Applicable."

5. Position/Decision: Must support position taken based on background and discussion.

7. Action Officer: 1stLt Brian Rafalski, S-2A, 450-0123

                              NIKOLAS LIDSTROM
                              Major, U.S. Marine Corps
                              (Section Head/Briefer)

DECISION MATRIX

OpsO Recommends: Approved _____

                             Disapproved _____

XO Recommends: Approved _____

                             Disapproved _____

CO Recommends: Approved _____

                             Disapproved _____

Classified by: _____
Declassify on: _____

Position Paper Guidelines

- Prepared by an action officer.

- Develops and recommends an official position on a particular issue.

- Includes a clear statement of why an official position is required.

- Provides rational for recommended position.

- Usually put together rapidly by the action officer, who must identify key sources of information pertaining to the topic.

- Action officer must make sound analysis and write the paper in a clear, accurate and efficient format.

- References can be included in the same format as a standard letter.

- Enclosures or attachments are authorized.

- Must have a Purpose paragraph that explains the issue to be discussed.

- A Decision block can be included as required for approval/disapproval.

- If document is classified, refer to MCO P5510.18, unit S-2 or Classified Material Control Center for proper marking and storage requirements.

UNITED STATES MARINE CORPS
1ST BATTALION, 6TH MARINES
2D MARINE DIVISION
PSC BOX 1775
CAMP LEJEUNE, NC 28542

28 Mar 10

TALKING PAPER

For use by LtCol Zetterberg

Subj: TALKING PAPER FORMAT

<u>Background</u>: Short, concise information about subject. Give the speaker a quick reference, bring up-to-date, i.e. Fallujah has been a haven for insurgents since 2003. Current intel provides four strongholds in town.

<u>Discussion</u>: Concise narrative of points related to topic. Can be bulletized for clarity/brevity.

    a. Fallujah is key to insurgent success.

    b. Can be considered the "head of the snake".

    c. Civilian population is leaving area.

<u>Recommendation</u>: Prepare a battle plan using combined arms to crush the insurgents in the town.

<u>Action Officer</u>: Maj Dan Cleary, S-3 Air, 450-1941

Classified by: _____
Declassify on: _____

Talking Paper Format

- Used to advance a point of view or summarize an action/proposal.

- Although points are concise, does not need to be bulletized.

- References are authorized and should be annotated as necessary.

- Should not require attachments or enclosures.

- Should be written by an action officer, capable of doing in-depth research on subject.

- Commonly used as a "memory tickler" for superior, or quick reference outline.

- Recommendations should be clear and succinct.

- Do not exceed two pages.

- If document is classified, refer to MCO P5510.18, unit S-2 or Classified Material Control Center for proper marking and storage requirements.

UNITED STATES MARINE CORPS
1ST BATTALION, 6TH MARINES
2D MARINE DIVISION
PSC BOX 1775
CAMP LEJEUNE, NC 28542

1900
S-1
7 Jan 10

LETTER OF INSTRUCTION 1-10

From: Commanding Officer
To: All Marines

Subj: LETTER OF INSTRUCTION (LOI) FOR RETIREMENT CEREMONY
       FOR MASTER GUNNERY SERGEANT STEVE YZERMAN

Ref: (a) Marine Corps Manual

Encl: (1) List of Key Personnel
       (2) Sequence of Events (Outdoor Ceremony)
       (3) Sequence of Events (Indoor Ceremony)

1. <u>Situation</u>. Per the reference, a retirement ceremony will
be held for Master Gunnery Sergeant Bret Hedican on 28 October
2006.

2. <u>Mission</u>. This unit will conduct the most motivating,
dynamic, and cutting edge retirement ceremony ever seen in the
history of the Marine Corps.

3. <u>Execution</u>

   a. <u>Commander's Intent and Concept of Operations</u>. My
intent is to provide the Marine and his family with a ceremony
worthy of his 30 years of service. The Sergeant Major will
ensure that all personnel in enclosure (1) are ready to
perform the ceremonies contained in enclosures (2) and (3).

   b. <u>Subordinate Element Missions</u>. 2d Battalion, 6th Marines
will provide security and drivers for this event.

   c. <u>Coordinating Instructions</u>. The Executive Officer will
ensure sections coordinate as necessary to accomplish this
mission.

4. <u>Administration and Logistics</u>

   a. <u>Administration</u>. S-1 will provide invitations, track
RSVP's, arrange for seating charts, programs and flowers.

LETTER OF INSTRUCTION 1-10

b. Logistics. S-4 will coordinate vehicle support, area
for parking, bus transportation for guests. Ensure adequate
food is arranged for guests. Bag nasties for Marines.
Coordinate with Aid Station for Corpsman to monitor Marines
in formation.

5. Command and Signal. Effective date signed and applies to
the hard-charging Marines of the finest battalion in the world!

                          CHRIS OSGOOD

Copy to:
2d Bn, 6th Mar, 2d MarDiv
6th Mar, 2d MarDiv

2

16

Letter of Instruction (LOI) Format

- Utilize LOI for coordinating one-time events, or providing commander's guidance on a particular item.

- Majority of format is based on standard letter (SECNAVINST 5216.5) and Marine Corps directives (MCO 5215.1).

- Utilize the 5 paragraph order format (SMEAC).

- Provide the information needed for instruction, but strive to be concise.

- Annotate references as needed.

- Enclosures are authorized and should be attached to the LOI when published.

- Ensure the underlined words LETTER OF INSTRUCTION X-XX are the top of each successive page, and the enclosures. LOI's are issued by calendar year, the first would be 1-(2 digit year), the second would be 2-(2 digit year).

- LOI's can be signed "Acting" or "By direction" if necessary, but should be issued directly from the commander.

- Recommendation is that unit prepares a "Letter of Instruction" binder, and keeps all originals in the binder. Alternate method of filing is in correspondence files.

UNITED STATES MARINE CORPS
1ST BATTALION, 6TH MARINES
2D MARINE DIVISION
PSC BOX 1775
CAMP LEJEUNE, NC 28542

1300
S-1
7 Apr 10

POLICY LETTER 3-10

From: Commanding Officer
To: All Marines

Subj: POLICY CONCERNING REQUESTS FOR SPECIAL DUTY ASSIGNMENTS

Ref: (a) MCO P1326.11B

Encl: (1) Financial Screening Checklist

1. Purpose. To establish policy for this unit for Marines
desiring to request special duty assignments.

2. Cancellation. This letter will remain in effect until
revision or when indicated by the appropriate authority.

3. Information. Reference (a) establishes procedures for
Marines desiring special duties, i.e. Drill Instructor, Marine
Security Guard, Recruiting or School of Infantry Instructor. The
policy for this command will be that these duty assignments are
encouraged, however, the mission of the unit supersedes the
desire of the Marine. Enclosure (1) must be completed by all
applicants.

   a. Drill Instructor Duty. Marines requesting this duty must
interview with the Sergeant Major.

   b. Recruiting Duty. Marines requesting this duty will
interview with the Division Career Planner for HRST screening.

   c. Marine Security Guard Duty. Marines requesting this
duty will be required to complete a security investigation at the
S-2 prior to submission.

   d. School of Infantry Duty. Marines requesting this duty
will see the Career Planner, and set up an appointment with the
Sergeant Major, School of Infantry East, Camp Geiger.

4. Scope. In order to ascertain the duty to which an individual
is best suited, and to ease the paperwork burden, the directions
in the above paragraphs must be carried out prior to an actual
request will be submitted. This will ensure no Marines depart
this battalion who are not totally prepared for the special duty.

5. __Certification.__   (If necessary, this and other paragraphs can be utilized.)

                                CHRIS CHELIOS

Copy to:
2d Bn, 6th Mar, 2d MarDiv
6th Mar, 2d MarDiv

Financial Screening Checklist

Name:

Grade:

Base Pay:

Monthly Allowances (BAH, BAS):

Special Duty Allowance (if applicable):

Expenses:

Is any left over:

Qualified/Unqualified

Enclosure (1)

Policy Letter Format

- The Policy Letter is written to provide the commander's guidance on policy within a particular unit.

- Majority of format is based on standard letter (SECNAVINST 5216.5) and Marine Corps directives (MCO 5215.1).

- Utilize paragraph titled as necessary to clearly convey the intent of the commander/establish the policy.

- Provide the information needed for instruction, but strive to be concise.

- Annotate references as needed.

- Enclosures are authorized and should be attached to the PL when published.

- Ensure the underlined words POLICY LETTER X-XX are the top of each successive page, and the enclosures. PL's are issued by calendar year, the first would be 1-(2 digit year), the second would be 2-(2 digit year).

- PL's should only be signed by the commander, due to the legal nature of establishing unit policy.

- Recommendation is that unit prepares a "Policy Letter" binder, and keeps all originals in the binder. Alternate method of filing is in correspondence files.

NJP AUTHORITY

Authority cannot be delegated.
Acting CO's may not NJP based solely on their "Acting" status.

Maximum Punishments that can be awarded by:

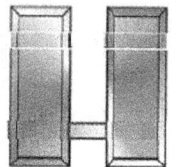

Company Grade CO's & All OIC's (regardless of grade) with
authority to NJP
MCM, 2008 edition, Part V, par 5b(2)(A) & UCMJ, Art 15(c),
pg A2-5

- Confinement on bread and water for 3 days (if embarked)
- CCU for 7 days
- Forfeiture of 7 days pay
- Extra duties for 14 days
- Restriction for 14 days

Field Grade (CO's only)
MCM, 2008 edition, Part V, par 5b(2)(B)

- Confinement on bread and water for 3 days
- CCU for 30 days
- Forfeiture of ½ months pay per month for 2 months
- Reduction one pay grade (Sgt and below only)
- Extra duties for 45 days
- Restriction for 60 days

Limitations on Punishments

- Corporal and above cannot receive CCU or confinement on bread and water unless reduced below Corporal at NJP
- Extra duties cannot be a known safety hazard and should only last 2 hours per day
- Reduce one rank at a time
- Restriction may not exceed maximum extra duties (45 days) if both are imposed

---

Refer to MCAAT web site for the maximum forfeiture chart.
https://www.manpower.usmc.mil

DEPARTMENT OF THE NAVY

MILITARY SUSPECT'S ACKNOWLEDGEMENT AND WAIVER OF RIGHTS

Place: _____

_____

I, _____

have been advised by _____

that I am suspected of _____

I have also been advised that:

(1) I have the right to remain silent and make no statement at all;

(2) Any statement I do make can be used against me in a trial by court-martial or other judicial or administrative proceeding;

(3) I have the right to consult with a lawyer prior to any questioning. This lawyer may be a civilian lawyer retained by me at no cost to the United States, a military lawyer appointed to act as my counsel at no cost to me, or both;

(4) I have the right to have my retained civilian lawyer and/or appointed military lawyer present during this interview; and

(5) I may terminate this interview at any time, for any reason.

I understand my rights as related to me and as set forth above. With that understanding, I have decided that I do not desire to remain silent, consult with a retained or appointed lawyer, or have a lawyer present at this time. I make this decision freely and voluntarily. No threats or promises have been made to me.

Signature: _____

Date & Time: _____

Witnessed: _____

_____

Date & Time: _____

At this time, I, _____

desire to make the following voluntary statement. This statement is made with an understanding of my rights as set forth above. It is made with no threats or promises having been extended to me.

OPNAV 5527/3 (DEC 1982)

23

CAPTAIN'S MAST/OFFICE HOURS GUIDE

(NOTE: The formalities prior to and at the termination of the captain's mast or office hours normally are determined by custom and tradition in the Navy and Marine Corps.)

CO: You are suspected of committing the following violation(s) of the Uniform Code of Military Justice:

_____   ____

_____

_____

You do not have to make any statement regarding the offense(s) of which you are accused or suspected and any statement made by you may be used as evidence against   you.

(Note: If it is reasonably foreseeable that the accused's statements during the captain's mast/office hours proceedings may be considered for introduction in evidence in a later court-martial, an explanation of rights and a waiver, in the format of Appendix A-1-m of   the JAG Manual, will have to be obtained from the accused, during the hearing, before proceeding further.)

CO: You are advised that a captain's mast/office hours is not a trial and that a determination of misconduct on your part is not a conviction by a court. Further, you are advised that the formal rules of evidence used in trials by court-martial do not apply at captain's mast/office hours.

CO: I have a statement signed by you acknowledging that you were fully advised of your legal rights pertaining at this hearing. (Note: This statement will be either JAGMAN Appendix A-1-b, A-1-c, or A-1-d.)

CO: Do you understand this statement and do you understand the rights explained therein?

ACC: _____.

CO: Do you have any questions about them or do you wish to make and requests?

ACC: _____.

_____.

CO: [To witness (if any are present)] What can you tell me about the accused's involvement in (these) (this) offense(s)?

WIT: _____.

OR

A-1-e(1)

24

CO: [To witness(es) who has/have previously provided written statement(s) when accused and CO both have copies of the statement(s).] Do you adopt your statement(s) as your testimony here today?

WIT: _____ .

CO: Do you have anything to add to or change in your statement?

WIT: _____ .

CO: (To accused) Would you like me to ask any further questions of this witness?

ACC: _____ .

CO: (After all witnesses are questioned) I have before me the following (documents) (statements) (other physical evidence) that will be considered by me. Have you been given the opportunity to examine them?

ACC: _____ .

CO: (If the answer is "no," offer the accused the opportunity to examine the evidence.)

CO: Is there anything that you wish to offer? (If the answer is "yes," permit the accused the opportunity to call his witnesses, make a personal statement in defense, and present other evidence.)

ACC: _____ .

CO: Are there any other witnesses you would like to call or any other evidence you would like to present?

ACC: _____ .

CO: Is there anything that you wish to offer that would lessen the seriousness of (this) (these) offense(s) or mitigate them?

ACC: _____ .

CO: (To witness) What can you tell me about (accused's name) performance of duty?

WIT: _____ .

CO: (To accused) Is there anything else you would like to present?

ACC: _____.

CO: I impose the following punishment:

_____.

My decision to impose this punishment was based on my determination that you committed the minor offenses of:

_____.

You are advised that you have the right to appeal this punishment to (identify the superior authority by name and organizational title). Your appeal must be made within a reasonable time-- which is normally 5 days. Following this hearing, _____ will advise you more fully of this right to appeal. Do you understand?

ACC: _____.

CO: You are dismissed.

A-1-c(3)

(CAPTAIN'S MAST) (OFFICE HOURS)
ACCUSED'S ACKNOWLEDGEMENT OF APPEAL RIGHTS

(CAPTAIN'S MAST) (OFFICE HOURS) ACCUSED'S ACKNOWLEDGEMENT
OF APPEAL RIGHTS

I, _____ _____, SSN _____,
(Name and grade of accused)

assigned or attached to _____, have been informed of the following facts concerning
my rights of appeal as a result of (captain's mast) (office hours) held on _____:

a. I have the right to appeal to (specify to whom the appeal should be addressed).

b. My appeal must be submitted within a reasonable time. Five working days, excluding weekends and holidays, after the punishment is imposed is normally considered a reasonable time, in the absence of unusual circumstances. Any appeal submitted thereafter may be rejected as not timely. If there are unusual circumstances which I believe will make it extremely difficult or not practical to submit an appeal within 5 working days, I should immediately advise the officer imposing punishment of such circumstances, and request an appropriate extension of time which to file my appeal.

c. The appeal must be in writing.

d. There are only two grounds for appeal; that is:

(1) The punishment was unjust, or

(2) The punishment was disproportionate to the offense(s) for which it was imposed.

e. If the punishment imposed included reduction from the pay grade of E-4 or above, or was in excess of: arrest in quarters for 7 days, correctional custody for 7 days, forfeiture of 7 days' pay, extra duties for 14 days, restriction for 14 days, then the appeal must be referred to a military lawyer for consideration and advice before action is taken on my appeal.

_____   _____
(Signature of Accused and Date)   (Signature of Witness and Date)

A-1-f

Distribution:

Original copy to SRB/OQR
Copy to CMPF, UNIT FILES,
MEMBER

1. OFFENSES (To include specific circumstances and the date and place of commission of the offense.)

Art. 112. Drunk on duty. Specifically, driving a govt veh, while under the influence of alcohol, during a phys trng session on 6 Jan 10, at COA, 1st Bn, 10th Mar, 2d MarDiv, CamLej.

2. I have been advised of and understand my rights under Article 31, UCMJ. I also have been advised of and understand my right to demand trial by court-martial in lieu of non-judicial punishment. I (do) (do not) demand trial and (will) (will not) accept non-judicial punishment subject to my right of appeal. I further certify that I (have) (have not) been given the opportunity to consult with a military lawyer, provided at no expense to me, prior to my decision to accept non-judicial punishment.

	(DATE)	2010/01/10	(Signature of accused)

3. The accused has been afforded these rights under Article 31, UCMJ, and the right to demand trial by court-martial in lieu of non-judicial punishment.

	(DATE)	2010/01/10	(Signature of immediate CO of accused)

4. BOOKER STATEMENT: I have been given the opportunity to consult with a lawyer, provided by the Government at no cost to me, in regard to a pending NJP for violation of Article (s) 112 of the UCMJ. I understand I have the right to refuse that NJP; I (do) (do not) choose to exercise that right. I further understand that acceptance of NJP does not preclude my command from taking other adverse administrative action against me.

	(DATE)	2010/01/09	(Signature)

5. UNAUTHORIZED ABSENCES (in excess of 24 hours) AND MARKS OF DESERTION

6. FINAL DISPOSITION TAKEN AND DATE
To be red to LCpl, E-3, forf of $500 pay per mo for 2 mos. Total forf $1000. Restr to the limits of place of mess. bil. du, and worship and most dir route to and fr w/o susp fr du for 14 das and extra du for 14 das, to run concurrently. 10 Jan 10.

7. SUSPENSION OF EXECUTION OF PUNISHMENT, IF ANY
10 Jan 10. Red to LCpl, E-3, 14 das restr and extra du fur 14 das, susp for 6 mos, at which time, unless sooner vacated, all susp will be rem w/o further act.

8. FINAL DISPOSITION TAKEN BY (Name, grade, title)

J. T. BIRD, Col. CO

9. Upon consideration of the facts and circumstances surrounding (this offense) (these offenses) and upon further consideration of the needs of military discipline in this command, I have determined the offense (s) involved herein to be minor and properly punishable under Article 15, UCMJ, such punishment to be that indicated.

10. DATE OF NOTICE TO ACCUSED OF FINAL DISPOSITION TAKEN.

(Signature of CO who took final disposition in 6)

2010/01/10

11. The accused has been advised of the right of appeal	12. Having been advised of and understanding my right of appeal, at this time I (intend) (do not intend) to file an appeal.	13. DATE OF APPEAL, IF ANY
2010/01/10		
(DATE) (Signature of CO who took final action in 9)	2010/01/10	Not Appealed.
	(DATE) (Signature of accused)	

14. DECISION ON APPEAL (IF APPEAL IS MADE), DATE THEREOF, AND SIGNATURE OF CO WHO MADE DECISION.	15. DATE OF NOTICE TO ACCUSED OF DECISION ON APPEAL.
(DATE) (Signature of CO making decision on appeal)	

16. REMARKS	17. Final administrative action, as appropriate, has been completed.
	UD# 0003 DTD 2010/01/10 INIT FJH

18. UNIT

COA, 1st Bn, 10th Mar, 2d MarDiv, CamLej

19. INDIVIDUAL (Last name, first name, middle initial)	20. GRADE	21. SSN
BURTON ALICE J	Cpl. E-4	XXX XX 1654

Designed using FormFlow 2.22, HQMC/ARDE, Apr 2002

28

DESERTER/ABSENTEE WANTED BY THE ARMED FORCES	1. DATE PREPARED *(YYYYMMDD)* 20100412	REPORT CONTROL SYMBOL DD-P&R(SA)1454

2. TO *(Local, State or Federal law enforcement authority as indicated by Military Deserter Information Point)* See Distribution List	3. FROM *(Organization or activity and place from which absent. If unauthorized absence occurs in transit, list old and new unit in Remarks)* Commanding Officer 1st Battalion, 10th Marines 2d Marine Division Camp Lejeune, NC 28542-0106	4. DISTRIBUTION CMC (PSL.) SRB PNOK

5. ABSENTEE IDENTIFICATION

a. NAME *(Last, First, Middle Initial)* Dickerson, John H.	b. GRADE/RANK/RATE Private, E-1	c. SEX M

d. RACE *(X one or more)*	e. ETHNICITY *(X one)*
☐ AMERICAN INDIAN/ ALASKA NATIVE ☐ NATIVE HAWAIIAN OR OTHER PACIFIC ISLANDER	☐ HISPANIC OR LATINO
☐ ASIAN ☐ WHITE	☒ NOT HISPANIC OR LATINO
☐ BLACK OR AFRICAN AMERICAN ☐ DECLINE TO RESPOND	☐ DECLINE TO RESPOND

f. PLACE OF BIRTH *(City, State, Country)* Dallas, TX, USA	g. DATE OF BIRTH *(YYYYMMDD)* 19851210	h. HEIGHT 69"	i. WEIGHT 195

j. EYE COLOR *(X one)*	k. HAIR COLOR *(X one)*
☐ BLACK ☐ GREEN ☐ VIOLET	☐ AUBURN ☒ BROWN ☐ SILVER
☐ BLUE ☐ GRAY	☐ BLACK ☐ GRAY ☐ WHITE
☐ BROWN ☒ HAZEL	☐ BLOND ☐ RED ☐ BALD

l. DIP CONTROL NUMBER Leave this blank	m. BRANCH OF SERVICE M	n. SOCIAL SECURITY NO. 000-00-9087	o. CITIZENSHIP US	p. MARITAL STATUS S

q. MILITARY OCCUPATION 3531, Motor Transport Operator	s. PERMANENT RESIDENCE ADDRESS *(Include ZIP Code)* 11279 Partridge Road Dallas, TX 75218
r. CIVILIAN OCCUPATION Truck Driver	

6. CURRENT ENLISTMENT	7. ENTRY INTO CURRENT PERIOD OF SERVICE	8. ATTACH PHOTOGRAPH *(if available)*
a. DATE *(YYYYMMDD)* 20090319	b. PLACE *(City and State)* Dallas, TX	a. DATE *(YYYYMMDD)* Same as 6a.	b. PLACE *(City and State)* Same as 6b.	

9. TIME OF ABSENCE	10. ADMINISTRATIVE DATE OF DESERTION *(YYYYMMDD)*
a. DATE *(YYYYMMDD)* 20100312	b. HOUR 0730	20100411

11. ESCAPED OR SENTENCED PRISONER *(X as applicable)*	12. DISCHARGE STATUS *(X as applicable)*
☐ YES IF "YES," SPECIFY CHARGE ☒ NO	a. DISCHARGED ☐ YES ☒ NO b. SUSPENDED ☐ YES ☒ NO

13. OPERATOR'S LICENSE

a. NUMBER 1231930	b. STATE TX	c. EXP. DATE *(YYYYMMDD)* 20110305

14. VEHICLE LICENSE

a. PLATE NO. IBDUMB	b. STATE TX	c. EXP. DATE *(YYYYMMDD)* 20101231	d. TYPE unknown

15. VEHICLE

a. VEHICLE IDENTIFICATION NUMBER ZXBC1592796	b. YEAR 2003	c. MAKE Toyota	d. MODEL Celica	e. STYLE 2 door	f. COLOR silver

16. RELATIVES AND/OR PERSONS KNOWN BY ABSENTEE *(If more space is needed, continue in Remarks or on a separate page, making reference to this item number.)*

a. NAME *(Last, First, Middle Initial)*	b. ADDRESS *(Include ZIP Code)*
(1) Dickerson, John A.	11279 Partridge Road, Dallas, TX 75218
(2) Dickerson, Judy G.	11279 Partridge Road, Dallas, TX 75218
(3)	
(4)	
(5)	

DD FORM 553, NOV 2002   PREVIOUS EDITION IS OBSOLETE.   Page 1 of 3 Pages

17. CERTIFICATION *(See Notes)*

The undersigned states: That he/she is a commissioned officer of the United States   Marine Corps   *(Military Department, presently*
assigned as the Commanding Officer,   1st Bn, 10th Mar, 2d MarDiv   *(Unit from which the alleged deserter absented himself or herself),*
and in the performance of official duties imposed by Department of Defense Directive 1325.2 and   MCO P5800.16
(Regulations of the Service concerned which implement DOD Directive 1325.2; e.g. Army Regulations 190-9 and 630-10), he/she has conducted an investigation into the status of   John H. Dickerson, Private   *(Name and rank of alleged deserter),* a member of the United States
Armed Forces serving on active duty with   1st Bn, 10th Mar, 2d MarDiv, USMC   *(Unit and Service from which*
the alleged deserter absented himself or herself) by questioning his/her unit cohorts; by examining and verifying the field service records of said
service member which reflect his/her duty status; by requesting the member's next of kin to urge his/her voluntary return to military control if
they are aware of his/her whereabouts; by inquiring to the fullest extent possible into the feasibility of other explanations of the member's
absence, to include sickness, injury, hospitalization, and confinement by civil law enforcement officials; and officially ordered diversion from
his/her unit of assignment by querying the member's losing unit (and en route temporary duty unit), the appropriate career management division,
the servicing replacement organization, and the servicing Military Personnel and Transportation Assistance Office (and *(See Note 1)*

N/A

That based on the aforesaid investigation, the undersigned has personal knowledge that, on or about   20100412   *(Date - YYYYMMDD),*
John H. Dickerson, Private   *(Name and rank of alleged deserter)* did, without authority and with intent to remain away
therefrom permanently, absent himself/herself from his/her unit/organization/place of duty, to wit (See item 3 above) located at *(See item 2)* in
violation of Section 885, Title 10, United States Code and he/she has remained continuously so absent until   20100412
(Date this statement is executed - YYYYMMDD). I state under penalty of perjury (under the laws of the United States of America/See Note 2) that
the foregoing is true and correct. Executed on   N/A   *(Date - YYYYMMDD).*

NOTES:
1. For use only when a servicemember fails to report to a gaining unit of assignment during a permanent change of station.
2. For use only when statement is executed outside the United States, its territories, possessions and commonwealths.

18. COMMANDING OFFICER

a. TYPED NAME *(Last, First, Middle initial)*	b. RANK	c. TITLE
Bird, James T.	Col	Commanding Officer

d. ORGANIZATION AND INSTALLATION	e. SIGNATURE *(All copies)*	f. DATE SIGNED *(YYYYMMDD)*
1st Bn, 10th Mar, 2d MarDiv, CamLej 28542		20100412

19. REMARKS *(List peculiar habits and traits of character; unusual mannerisms and speech. Peculiarities in appearance; clothing worn, alias (names); marks and scars; tattoos; facial characteristics; complexion, posture, build, other SSN's used by individual; or other data that may assist in identification.*

- CONFIRMED MARIJUANA USER
- 8 YEARS MARTIAL ARTS EXPERIENCE
- has heart-shaped birthmark on the inside of his right calf
- USMC tattoo on right calf

If the Marine is considered an escape risk, pending charges or under investigation for violations of the UCMJ other than unauthorized absence or desertion, dangerous to him/herself or others, a violator of previous stragglers orders, or drug or alcohol addicted, appropriate cautionary statements will be placed in the remarks section of the DD Form 553 in CAPITAL LETTERS.

1. AUTHORITY TO APPREHEND.

a. Any civil officer having the authority to apprehend offenders under the laws of the United States, or of a State, territory, commonwealth, possession, or the District of Columbia may summarily apprehend deserters from the Armed Forces of the United States and deliver them into custody of military officials. Receipt of this form and a corresponding entry in the FBI's NCIC Wanted Person File, or oral notification from military officials or Federal law enforcement officials that the person has been declared a deserter and that his/her return to military control is desired, is authority for apprehension.

b. Civil authorities may apprehend absentees (AWOL's) when requested to do so by military authorities.

2. PAYMENT OF REWARD OR REIMBURSEMENT FOR EXPENSES.

a. Rewards. Receipt of this form, or oral or written notification from military authorities or Federal law enforcement officials, prior to apprehension of the individual, that the person is an absentee and that his/her return to military control is desired will be considered as an offer of reward. Persons or agency representatives (except salaried officers or employees of the Federal Government or servicemembers) apprehending or delivering absentees to military control are authorized:

(1) Payment for apprehension and detention of absentees until military authorities assume custody; or

(2) Payment for apprehension and delivery of absentees to a military installation.

b. Reimbursement for Expenses. Reimbursement may be made for actual expenses incurred when conditions for payment of a reward cannot be met. If two or more persons perform these services, payment will be made jointly or severally, but total payment to all may not exceed prescribed limitations.

c. Payment. Payment will be made to the person or agency representative actually making arrest and detention or delivery by the disbursing officer servicing the military facility to which the absentee is delivered and will be in full satisfaction of all expenses of apprehending, keeping and delivering the absentee. Payment may be made whether the absentee surrenders or is apprehended. Payment will not be made for information leading to apprehension, nor for apprehension not followed by return to military control. Both reward and reimbursement may not be paid for the same apprehension and detention or delivery.

3. INDIVIDUAL CLAIMS HE/SHE IS NOT ABSENT WITHOUT AUTHORITY.

When a detained individual claims that he/she is not absent without leave and does not have the papers to prove his/her claim, the apprehending person or agency representative should communicate directly by the most rapid means available, with the nearest military installation manned by active duty personnel. When necessary, communicate directly (telephone or telegraph) with the Deserter Information Point of the military service concerned.

a. US Army:		USAEREC, United States Army Deserter Information Point (UDADIP) 8899 East 56th Street Indianapolis, IN 46249-5301
	Telephone collect:	Area Code (317) 510-3711
b. US Navy:		Navy Absentee Collection and Information Center (NACIC) 2834 Greenbay Road North Chicago, IL 60064
	Telephone collect:	Area Code (847) 688-2106 (or toll free: 1-800-423-7633)
c. US Marine Corps:		Commandant, US Marine Corps Code POS-40 2 Navy Annex Washington, DC 20380-1775
	Telephone collect:	Area Code (703) 614-3248/3376
d. US Air Force:		Headquarters AF Personnel Center (DPWCM) 550 C Street West, Suite 14 Randolph AFB, TX 78150-4716
	Telephone collect:	Area Code (210) 566-3752 (or toll free: 1-800-531-5501)

REPORT OF RETURN OF ABSENTEE	REPORT CONTROL SYMBOL
	DD-P&R(SA)1454

IMPORTANT NOTICE

The absentee status of the individual named below has been terminated. Military records indicate that your agency was specifically furnished a copy of DD Form 553, "Deserter/Absentee Wanted by the Armed Forces," soliciting your support. Request you clear your records of the DD Form 553 pertaining to this individual and the associated unauthorized absence indicated on this report. The Department of Defense and the Military Service law enforcement officials concerned gratefully acknowledge your participation and support of military apprehension programs.

1. DISTRIBUTION (Same as DD Form 553 at time of absence)

CMC (PSL)
SRB
PNOK

2. NAME OF ABSENTEE (Last, First, Middle Initial)

Dickerson, John H.

3. SERVICE	4. SOCIAL SECURITY NO.	5. GRADE OR RATE
M	XXX XX 9087	Private, E-1

6. FORMER ABSENTEE STATUS

a. FORMER STATUS (X one)		b. DATE/HOUR ABSENCE BEGAN (YYYYMMDD)
(1) ESCAPED OR SENTENCED PRISONER	(2) ABSENTEE	20100312, 0730
	X (3) DESERTER (Administrative)	

c. ORGANIZATION AND INSTALLATION FROM WHICH ABSENT

1st Battalion, 10th Marines
2d Marine Division, Camp Lejeune, NC 28542

7. CIRCUMSTANCES OF ABSENTEE'S RETURN

a. MODE OF RETURN (X one)	b. AUTHORITIES TO WHOM ABSENTEE SURRENDERED OR BY WHOM APPREHENDED (X one)			
(1) APPREHENDED	X (1) MILITARY	(2) CIVIL	(3) FBI	(4) OIS
X (2) SURRENDERED	(5) OTHER (Specify)			

c. PLACE OF INITIAL RETURN	d. DATE/HOUR OF INITIAL RETURN (YYYYMMDD)
1st Battalion, 10th Marines 2d Marine Division, Camp Lejeune, NC 28542	20100425, 0240

e. REQUIRED ACTION (X one)			
X (1) RETURN TO MILITARY CONTROL	(2) RETAINED BY CIVIL AUTHORITIES	(3) CIVIL CHARGES	(4) SAFEKEEPING

f. MILITARY ORGANIZATION AND INSTALLATION OR CIVILIAN LOCATION	g. DATE RETURNED TO MILITARY CONTROL (YYYYMMDD)
1st Battalion, 10th Marines 2d Marine Division, Camp Lejeune, NC 28542	20100425

8. DISPOSITION OF ABSENTEE

a. ACTION BY MILITARY AUTHORITIES (X one)		b. TO (Name of Command in charge of absentee)	c. COST OF TRANSPORTATION (To be charged to the individual's account)
X (1) RETAINED	(2) TRANSFERRED	1st Battalion, 10th Marines 2d Marine Division, Camp Lejeune, NC 28542	$ 0.00
(3) TECHNICAL ARREST ORDERS	(4) GUARD		

9. REMARKS (Include location of Service, Pay and Health Records)

Original service record is missing. Temporary SRB, HR and DR are held by parent command.

10. AUTHORIZING OFFICIAL

a. TYPED NAME (Last, First, Middle Initial)	b. GRADE	c. TITLE
Bird, James T.	Col	Commanding Officer

d. ORGANIZATION	e. SIGNATURE (Sign all copies)	f. DATE SIGNED (YYYYMMDD)
1st Bn, 10th Mar, 2d MarDiv CamLei 28542		20100412

DD FORM 616, DEC 1999   PREVIOUS EDITION IS OBSOLETE.

CONFINEMENT ORDER

1. PERSON TO BE CONFINED			2. DATE (YYYYMMDD)

a. NAME (Last, First, Middle)
Carbon, Tommy C.

b. SSN
000-00-6789

2. DATE (YYYYMMDD)
20100314

c. BRANCH OF SERVICE
USMC

d. GRADE
Pvt/E-1

e. MILITARY ORGANIZATION (From):
PAScol, MCCSSS, TrngCmd, CamLej

TYPE OF CONFINEMENT

3.a. PRE-TRIAL [ ] NO [X] YES   **b. RESULT OF NJP** [X] NO [ ] YES

c. RESULT OF COURT MARTIAL: [X] NO [ ] YES

TYPE: [ ] SCM [X] SPCM [ ] GCM [ ] VACATED SUSPENSION

d. DNA PROCESSING [ ] IS [X] IS NOT REQUIRED UNDER 10 U.S.C. 1565.

4. OFFENSES/CHARGES OF UCMJ ARTICLES VIOLATED:
Chg I: Art 86, Spec 1: UA 2145, 051217 - 0930, 100118, Spec 2: UA 0900, 100124 - Apprehended 1200, 100311
Chg II: Art 92, Spec: Disobeyed a superior commissioned officer

5. SENTENCE ADJUDGED:

b. ADJUDGED DATE (YYYYMMDD):

6. IF THE SENTENCE IS DEFERRED, THE DATE DEFERMENT IS TERMINATED:

7. PERSON DIRECTING CONFINEMENT

a. TYPED NAME, GRADE AND TITLE:
J. T. MULLINS, Col, Commanding Officer

b. SIGNATURE

c. DATE (YYYYMMDD)
20100314

d. TIME
07:30

8.a. NAME, GRADE, TITLE OF LEGAL REVIEW AND APPROVAL

b. SIGNATURE:

c. DATE (YYYYMMDD)

MEDICAL CERTIFICATE

9a. The above named inmate was examined by me at __12:00__ (Time) on __20100314__ (YYYYMMDD) and found to be [X] Fit [ ] Unfit for confinement. I certify that from this examination the execution of the foregoing sentence to confinement [ ] will [X] will not produce serious injury to the inmate's health.

b. The following irregularities were noted during the examination (If none, so state):
None.

c. HIV Test administered on (YYYYMMDD): __20100314__

d. Pregnancy test administered on (YYYYMMDD): __ [X] N/A

10. EXAMINER

a. TYPED NAME, GRADE AND TITLE:
S. E. STEVENS, LT, MedO

b. SIGNATURE

c. DATE (YYYYMMDD)
20100314

d. TIME
12:00

RECEIPT FOR INMATE

11.a. THE INMATE NAMED ABOVE HAS BEEN RECEIVED FOR CONFINEMENT AT: MCB BRIG CAMLEJ
(Facility Name and Location)
ON __20100314__ (YYYYMMDD) AND TIME: 16:00 (Time)

b. PERSON RECEIPTING FOR INMATE TYPED NAME, GRADE AND TITLE:
W. C. SANDERS, GySgt, NCOIC

c. SIGNATURE:

d. DATE (YYYYMMDD)
20100314

e. TIME
16:00

DD F **SECNAVIST 1640.9 is the reference used to complete the Confinement Order** fessional 6.0

CONFINEMENT ORDER

1. PERSON TO BE CONFINED

		2. DATE *(YYYYMMDD)*
a. NAME *(Last, First, Middle)* Carbon, Tommy C.	**b. SSN** 000-00-6789	20100314

c. BRANCH OF SERVICE USMC	**d. GRADE** Pvt/E-1	**e. MILITARY ORGANIZATION** *(From)*: PAScol, MCCSSS, TrngCmd, CamLej

TYPE OF CONFINEMENT

3.a. PRE-TRIAL [X] NO   [ ] YES   **b. RESULT OF NJP** [X] NO   [ ] YES

c. RESULT OF COURT MARTIAL: [ ] NO   [X] YES

TYPE: [ ] SCM   [X] SPCM   [ ] GCM   [ ] VACATED SUSPENSION

d. DNA PROCESSING [ ] IS   [X] IS NOT REQUIRED UNDER 10 U.S.C. 1565.

4. OFFENSES/CHARGES OF UCMJ ARTICLES VIOLATED:
Chg I: Art 86, Spec 1: UA 2145, 051217 - 0930,

5. SENTENCE ADJUDGED: BCD, 90 das cnft, forf $450 pay per mo for 2 mos	**b. ADJUDGED DATE** *(YYYYMMDD)*: 20100314

6. IF THE SENTENCE IS DEFERRED, THE DATE DEFERMENT IS TERMINATED:

7. PERSON DIRECTING CONFINEMENT

a. TYPED NAME, GRADE AND TITLE: J. T. MULLINS, Col, Commanding Officer	**b. SIGNATURE**	**c. DATE** *(YYYYMMDD)* 20100314	**d. TIME** 07:30

8.a. NAME, GRADE, TITLE OF LEGAL REVIEW AND APPROVAL U. R. BUSTED, Capt, Trial Counsel	**b. SIGNATURE:**	**c. DATE** *(YYYYMMDD)* 20100314

MEDICAL CERTIFICATE

9a. The above named inmate was examined by me at ___12:00___ on ___20100314___ and found to be [X] Fit [ ] Unfit
                                (Time)   *(YYYYMMDD)*
for confinement. I certify that from this examination the execution of the foregoing sentence to confinement
[ ] will   [X] will not produce serious injury to the inmate's health.

b. The following irregularities were noted during the examination *(If none, so state)*:
None.

c. HIV Test administered on *(YYYYMMDD)*:   20100314

d. Pregnancy test administered on *(YYYYMMDD)*:   [X] N/A

10. EXAMINER

a. TYPED NAME, GRADE AND TITLE: S. E. STEVENS, LT, MedO	**b. SIGNATURE**	**c. DATE** *(YYYYMMDD)* 20100314	**d. TIME** 12:00

RECEIPT FOR INMATE

11.a. THE INMATE NAMED ABOVE HAS BEEN RECEIVED FOR CONFINEMENT AT: MCB BRIG CAMLEJ
(Facility Name and Location)

ON ___20100314___ AND TIME: ___16:00___
   (YYYYMMDD)   *(Time)*

b. PERSON RECEIPTING FOR INMATE TYPED NAME, GRADE AND TITLE: W. C. SANDERS, GySgt, NCOIC	**c. SIGNATURE:**	**d. DATE** *(YYYYMMDD)* 20100314	**e. TIME** 16:00

DD F SECNAVIST 1640.9 is the reference used to complete the Confinement Order *fessional 6.0*

PAGE 11 ENTRIES

ALCOHOL ABUSE   (PG 4-51 of MCO P1070.12)

YYYYMMDD. Counseled this date concerning my conviction of_____ .

Recommendations for corrective action are _____ .

Assistance is available from _____ .

I am advised that failure to take corrective action may result in
administrative separation or limitation on further service. I was
advised that within 5 working days after acknowledgment of this
entry a written rebuttal could be submitted and that such a
rebuttal will be filed on the documents side of the service
record. I choose (to) (not to) make such a statement.

_____ SNM _____ Bydir

ADMINISTRATIVE SEPARATION COUNSELING (6105) (PG 4-53 of MCO P1070.12)

YYYYMMDD. Counseled this date concerning deficiencies_____ .

Recommendations for corrective action are _____ .

Assistance is available from _____ .

I am advised that failure to take corrective action may result in
administrative separation or limitation on further service. I was
advised that within 5 working days after acknowledgment of this
entry a written rebuttal can be submitted and this rebuttal will
be filed on the document side of the SRB. I choose (to) (not to)
make a rebuttal.

_____ SNM _____ CO

ELIGIBLE BUT NOT RECOMMENDED FOR PROMOTION (PG 4-48 of MCO P1070.12)

YYYYMMDD. I understand I am eligible but not recommended for
promotion to _____ for the _____ promotion period because
_____ . I was advised that within 5 working days
after acknowledgment of this entry, a written rebuttal can be
submitted and this rebuttal will be filed on the document side of
my SRB. I choose (to) (not to) make a rebuttal.

SNM

UNITED STATES MARINE CORPS
1ST BATTALION, 10TH MARINES
2D MARINE DIVISION
PSC BOX 20106
CAMP LEJEUNE, NC 28542-0041

IN REPLY REFER TO:
5800
Adj
31 Jan 10

From: Commanding Officer
To: First Lieutenant James T. Jones XXX XX 9876/0802 USMC

Subj: PUNITIVE LETTER OF REPRIMAND

Ref: (a) UCMJ Art. 15
        (b) Para. 5 of Part V, MCM 2008
        (c) JAGMAN 0114

1. Reference (a) is the record of an investigation convened by the Commanding Officer, 1st Battalion, 10th Marines, to inquire into the circumstances of a government vehicle accident that occurred on 15 December 2009. The accident occurred on Hwy 172 about 20 miles east of Camp Lejeune, North Carolina. You were a party to the investigation and were accorded your rights as such. You have been advised that you have the right to refuse imposition of nonjudicial punishment and you have elected to accept nonjudicial punishment.

2. You were negligent in the proper safety of the passengers on the 7 ton vehicle which you were convoy leader. Your disregard to standing operating procedures and base regulations are apparent when the vehicle was exceeding the posted speed limit and a passenger was thrown from the vehicle.

3. Your actions clearly show that you were derelict in the performance of your duties as convoy leader on the morning of 15 December 2009 in that you negligently failed to:

    a. Ensure that each vehicle operator was properly briefed on maintaining the posted speed limit and ensuring that all safety restraints were in place as required by Battalion Order 3510.1.

    b. Informing your commanding officer when a member of the command was injured as required by Battalion Order 1000.12.

                            J. T. BIRD

UNITED STATES MARINE CORPS
1st BATTALION, 10th MARINES
2D MARINE DIVISION
PSC BOX 20106
CAMP LEJEUNE, NC 28542-0041

IN REPLY REFER TO:
5800
Adj
31 Jan 10

From: Commanding Officer
To: Sergeant John D. Smith XXX XX 6789/0411 USMC

Subj: NONPUNITIVE LETTER OF CAUTION

Ref: (a) Report of investigation into Equal Opportunity Complaint, dtd
          20100115
      (b) R.C.M. 306, MCM 2008
      (c) JAGMAN 0105

1. Reference (a) is the record of investigation by Capt John H. Doe to inquire into an equal opportunity complaint made against you on 15 January 2010.

2. (Here insert a precise statement of the relevant events and circumstances for which the letter of caution is being issued.) From the forgoing, it is apparent that your behavior was inappropriate and offensive. Such behavior is contrary to Marine Corps policy and regulation and is detrimental to the esprit de corps, pride and readiness of every Marine and/or this command. Accordingly, you are hereby administratively cautioned pursuant to references (b) and (c).

3. This letter, being nonpunitive, is addressed to you as a corrective measure. It does not become a part of your official record. You are advised, however, that in the future you will be expected to exercise greater pride in your behavior in order to measure up to the high standard of conduct required by all members of the Marine Corps team. I trust the instructional benefit which you will receive from the experience will cause you to become a more professional Marine.

J. T. BIRD

Manual of the Judge Advocate General (JAGMAN) JAG Instruction 5800.7 is the reference used to complete Punitive Letters of Caution.

Minimum TIG/TIS Requirements

| USMC & USMCR | REGULAR PROMOTION | | MERITORIOUS PROMOTION | |
PROMOTION TO	TIG	TIS	TIG	TIS
SgtMaj/MGySgt	3 YRS	10 YRS	- -	- - -
1stSgt	4 YRS	8 YRS	- -	- - -
MSgt	4 YRS	8 YRS	N/A	8 YRS
GySgt	3 YRS	6 YRS	N/A	6 YRS
SSgt	27 MOS	4 YRS	N/A	4 YRS
Sgt	12 MOS	24 MOS	N/A	18 MOS
Cpl	8 MOS	12 MOS	N/A	6 MOS
LCpl	8 MOS	9 MOS	N/A	NONE
PFC	6 MOS	6 MOS	N/A	NONE

MCO P1400.32 (Enlisted Promotion Manual) is the reference for minimum time
in grade (TIG) and time in service (TIS) requirements.

The below schedule indicates the cutoff date for input of data elements, the
approximate date that composite scores will be computed, and the months the
composite scores for each quarter are reflected on the unit's Diary Feedback
Report (DFR) for each regular promotion quarter:

| | MCTFS CS Data | CS Months | CS is |
Promotion Quarter	Elements Cutoff	Computed*	On Unit DFR
Jan, Feb, Mar	20 November	30 November	Dec, Jan, Feb
Apr, May, Jun	20 February	28 February	Mar, Apr, May
Jul, Aug, Sep	20 May	31 May	Jun, Jul, Aug
Oct, Nov, Dec	20 August	31 August	Sep, Oct, Nov

* Composite scores for each regular and reserve promotion quarter are
computed approximately 5-10 days after the "MCTFS CS Data Elements Cutoff".

MCO P1400.32 (Enlisted Promotion Manual) is the reference for cutoff times.

Composite Score Worksheet

Line Number   **Rating**

1. Rifle Marksmanship Score _____   _____   _____ (Date of qual YYMMDD)

2. PFT/CFT Score _____   _____   _____ (Date of test YYMMDD)

3. Subtotal (line 1 + 2)   _____

4. GMP Score (line 3 divided by 2)   _____   Score

5. GMP Score (from line 4) x 100   _____   _____

6. Average Duty Proficiency ___ x 100   _____   _____

7. Average Conduct _____ x 100   _____   _____

8. TIG (months) ___ x 5   _____   _____

9. TIS (months) _____ x 2   _____   _____
   (computed from AFADBD for USMC and Active
   Reserve and from PEBD for Drilling Reserve)

10. DI/Recruiter/MSG Bonus/ ___ x 1   _____   _____
    1st term reenl (60)

11. Self-Education Bonus:
    (maximum of 100 points)

    a. MCI/Extension School ___ x15   _____   _____

    b. College/CLEP/Vocational ___ x10   _____   _____

12. Command Recruiting Bonus ___ x 20   _____   _____
    (maximum of 100 points)

13. Composite Score (sum of lines 5 to 12)   _____

MCO P1400.32 (Enlisted Promotions Manual) is the reference for completing
the Composite Score Worksheet

Promotion Restrictions

Marines will not be promoted while in any of the following categories:

- Within 18 months of the date convicted by a general court-martial. Commanders may partially waive this restriction, in the cases of exceptionally well-qualified Marines in the grades of Pvt and PFC, 12 months after the date of conviction.

- Within 12 months of the date convicted by a special court-martial. Commanders may partially waive this restriction, in the cases of exceptionally well-qualified Marines in the grades of Pvt and PFC, 6 months after the date of conviction if the Marine meets minimum TIG/TIS requirements.

- Within 6 months of the date convicted by a summary court-martial.

- In a probationary status as the result of sentence by a court-martial.

- Within 3 months of the date awarded nonjudicial punishment. In the case where Marine is awarded a punitive reduction (to Pvt through Cpl), the Marine must also serve the full time in grade requirement inclusively before becoming eligible for promotion. Paragraphs 2101.1a(4), 2101.2a(4) 2102.1a(4), 2102.2a(4), 2201.1b(2), 2201.2b(2), and 2202.10b apply.

- In a probationary status as a result of NJP under the authority of the UCMJ, Article 15, where any portion of the punishment is suspended. Commanders may partially waive this restriction, in the cases of exceptionally well-qualified Marines in the grades of Pvt and PFC, 3 months after the date of conviction.

- Within 12 months of an administrative reduction to Sgt or higher grade as a result of a Competency Review Board (CRB).

- Within 6 months of a punitive or administrative reduction to LCpl or Cpl as a result of a CRB.

- Within 3 months of a punitive or administrative reduction to Pvt or PFC as a result of a CRB.

- While in a suspended administrative reduction status as a result of a CRB. Commanders may partially waive this restriction, in the cases of exceptionally well-qualified Marines in the grades of Pvt and PFC, 3 months after the CRB is approved.

- Within 18 months of the date confirmed distribution, use or possession of illegal drugs took place. For purposes of this paragraph, the 18-month period will begin on the date positive confirmation is received from the DoD certified drug testing laboratory in the case of urinalysis detection, or from the date of the illegal drug incident, or other means of identification resulting in a conviction or finding of guilt.

NOTE: This promotion restriction does take precedence over the restrictions contained in paragraphs 1204.4g, 1204.4h, and 1204.4j.

- Within 12 months of conviction by military (to include a military magistrate) or civil authorities of Driving Under the Influence (DUI) or Driving While Intoxicated (DWI). Commanders may partially waive this restriction in the cases of exceptionally well qualified Marines in the grades of PFC and Pvt to 6 months after the date of conviction.

- Within 6 months of conviction by civil authorities (foreign or domestic), or action taken which is tantamount to a finding of guilt, i.e. a plea of no contest, for an offense which is considered a misdemeanor, other than minor traffic violations, in the civil jurisdiction. This restriction will apply to any traffic violation that is considered a misdemeanor and is punishable by law, i.e. reckless driving. Commanders are required to submit copies of court documentation evidencing the nature and degree of the offense, i.e. misdemeanor, felony, etc.

- Marines pending administrative separation for misconduct, unsatisfactory participation in the reserve component, homosexual conduct, unsatisfactory performance, alcohol rehabilitation failure, domestic violence, child abuse, weight control failure, etc. are not eligible for selection consideration or promotion. The loss of promotion eligibility begins the date the administrative separation package is signed by the commander for forwarding to the General Court-Martial Convening Authority for final disposition.

NOTE: This includes medical separations determined to be not in the line of duty or due to a member's own misconduct.

- While serving under a suspended administrative discharge.

- While assigned to the Body Composition Program (BCP).

- After failure of the semi-annual Marine Corps Physical Fitness Test (PFT). This restriction remains in effect until the Marine passes the PFT.

- While awaiting a pending court-martial or nonjudicial punishment.

- While pending adjudication of charges by a civil court, either foreign or domestic.

- When not recommended for reenlistment. (Reenlistment Code (RE) RE-4/4B)

- When assigned an RE-3C/3P for substandard performance. The RE-3C reenlistment code assigned in conjunction with a humanitarian transfer is not a promotion restriction.

- While in a probationary status as a result of a civilian conviction where any portion of the punishment is suspended. Commanders may partially waive this restriction, in the case of exceptionally qualified Marines in the grades of Pvt and PFC, 3 months after the date of conviction.

- While attending mandatory rehabilitation for any Level III, IV, or V Domestic Violence or Child Abuse offense.

Proficiency and Conduct Occasion Codes

	Code	
Occasions	Regular	Reserve
Transfer	TR	TR
Assignment to active duty		
Assignment to Involuntary Active Duty (Reserve)		
Release from active duty		
Release from EAD, AR, etc (Reserve)		
Completion of Initial Skill Training		
Completion of recruit training		
Temporary Disability Retired List (TDRL)	DL	DL
Discharge	DC	DC
Promotion to Corporal or Sergeant	PR	PR
Reduction	RD	RD
Declared Deserter (first day of UA period)	DD	--
Last day prior to declaring deserter	PD	--
To TAD	TD	--
TAD Complete	TC	--
Change of Primary duty	CD	CD
Service School Completion	SC	SC
Semiannual	SA	--
Annual	--	AN
Completion of Annual Training (Reserve)	--	AT
Recommended (See MCO P1400.32)	RE	RE
ADOS (Active Duty for Operational Support)	--	RT

If the effective date of transfer (TR) marks coincide with the requirement to report semiannual (SA) marks, TR marks will take precedence.

MCO P1070.12 (IRAM) is the reference for assigning Proficiency and Conduct Marks

MARK	CORRESPONDING ADJECTIVE RATING	STANDARDS OF CONDUCT
0.0 to 1.9	Unacceptable	Habitual offender. Conviction by general, special, or more than one summary court-martial. Give a mark of "0" upon declaration of desertion. Ordered to confinement pursuant to sentence of court-martial. Two or more punitive reductions in grade.
2.0 to 2.9	Unsatisfactory	No special court-martial. Not more than one summary court-martial. Not more than two nonjudicial punishments. Punitive reduction in grade.
3.0 to 3.9	Below Average	No court-martial. Not more than one nonjudicial punishment. No favorable impression of the qualities listed in paragraph 4007.6a. Failure to make satisfactory progress while assigned to the weight control or military appearance program. Conduct such as not to impair appreciably one's usefulness or the efficiency of the command, but conduct not sufficient to merit an honorable discharge.
4.0 to 4.4	Average	No offenses. No unfavorable impressions as to attitude, interests, cooperation, obedience, after-effects of intemperance, courtesy and consideration, and observance of regulations.
4.5 to 4.8	Excellent	No offense. Positive favorable impressions of the qualities listed in paragraph 4007.6a. Demonstrates reliability, good influence, sobriety, obedience, and industry.
4.9 to 5.0	Outstanding	No offenses. Exhibits to an outstanding degree the qualities listed in paragraph 4007.6a. Observes spirit as well as letter of orders and regulations. Demonstrates positive effect on others by example and persuasion.

4-41

MARK	CORRESPONDING ADJECTIVE RATING	STANDARDS OF PROFICIENCY
0.0 to 1.9	Unacceptable	Does unacceptable work in most duties, generally undependable; needs considerable assistance and close supervision on even the simplest assignment.
2.0 to 2.9	Unsatisfactory	Does acceptable work in some of the duties but cannot be depended upon. Needs assistance and close supervision on all but the simplest assignments.
3.0 to 3.9	Below Average	Handles routine matters acceptably but needs close supervision when performing duties not of a routine nature.
4.0 to 4.4	Average	Can be depended upon to discharge regular duties thoroughly and competently but usually needs assistance in dealing with problems not of a routine nature.
4.5 to 4.8	Excellent	Does excellent work in all regular duties, but needs assistance in dealing with extremely difficult or unusual assignments.
4.9 to 5.0	Outstanding	Does superior work in all duties. Even extremely difficult or unusual assignments can be given with full confidence that they will be handled in a thoroughly competent manner.

PERFORMANCE EVALUATION SYSTEM

APPENDIX A

ANNUAL FITNESS REPORT SCHEDULE (AN AND AR REPORTS)

GRADE OF	REPORTING PERIOD ENDS LAST DAY OF ACTIVE COMPONENT	REPORTING PERIOD ENDS LAST DAY OF RESERVE COMPONENT	REPORTING PERIODS ENDS LAST DAY OF ACTIVE RESERVE
SGT	MAR	SEP	SEP
SSGT	DEC	SEP	SEP
GYSGT	JUN	SEP	SEP
1STSGT/MSGT	JUN	SEP	SEP
SGTMAJ/MGYSGT	SEP	MAY	JUN
WO/CWO	APR	OCT	OCT
2NDLT	JAN/JUL	APR	N/A
1STLT	OCT/APR	OCT	OCT
CAPT	MAY	SEP	JUN
MAJ	MAY	SEP	JUN
LTCOL	MAY	JUN	JUN
COL	MAY	JUL	JUL
BGEN	JUN	JUN	N/A

1. All reports for Marines should arrive at HQMC no later than 30 days after the reporting period to ensure proper processing into official records to facilitate selection board and personnel management decisions.

2. Reserve members who are considered for promotion by an Active Component selection board will receive AN reports while those who are considered by a Reserve Component selection board (to include Active Reserve Marines) will receive AR reports.

3. Reports on Active Component 2nd and 1st lieutenants are semiannual (SA) vice annual (AN).

APPENDIX I

REENLISTMENT CODES

Code	When Assigned	Remarks
RE-1A	Recommended and eligible	No restriction to reenlistment. Meets all prerequisites, includes those Marines discharged at EAS while pregnant who would otherwise be eligible.
RE-1B	Recommended, eligible and requested retention but denied retention by CMC. May only be assigned by CMC.	For corporals/sergeants/staff sergeant with satisfactory performance records released at EAS due to ECFC.
RE-1C	Recommended and eligible career Marines meeting generally acceptable standards and denied further service.	Assigned by CMC to career Marines requesting retention who are eligible for retention, meet generally acceptable standards, and are denied further service by CMC.
RE-2A	Transferred to the FMCR.	Voluntary transfer to the FMCR. SPD will denote eligibility for reenlistment and whether at service limitations.
RE-2B	Retired.	Not eligible for reenlistment. For disability or transfer to the TDRL assign RE-3P.
RE-2C	Transferred to FMCR at maximum service limitation for grade	Not eligible for reenlistment at time of transfer to FMCR
RE-3A	Failure to meet general technical score prerequisite. Assign when single disqualifying factor.	Recommended by CO upon removal of disqualifying factor. SRB entry required stating reason for assignment. Individual Marine must sign SRB entry. CMC authority required for reenlistment.
RE-3B	Assign when there is a military or civil record of in-service illegal drug involvement before 31 Aug 92 and there is potential for further service.	SRB entry required stating reason for assignment. Individual Marine must sign SRB entry. CMC authority required for for further service.

REENLISTMENT CODES

Code	When Assigned	Remarks
RE-3C	When directed by CMC or when not eligible and disqualifying factor is not covered by any other code.	SRB entry required stating reason for assignment. Individual Marine must sign SRB entry. CMC authority required for reenlistment.
RE-3E	Failure to meet education standards. Assign when single disqualifying factor only.	Recommended by CO upon removal of disqualifying factor. SRB entry required stating reason for assignment. Individual Marine must sign SRB entry. CMC authority required for reenlistment.
RE-3F	Failure to complete recruit training.	SRB entry required stating reason for assignment, to include women Marines discharged due to pregnancy prior to completing recruit training. Individual Marine must sign SRB entry. CMC authority required for reenlistment.
RE-3H	Hardship discharge.	Assign when discharged pursuant to paragraph 6407. SRB entry required stating reason for assignment. Individual Marine must sign SRB entry. CMC authority required for reenlistment.
RE-3N	Pregnancy, single parenthood.	A woman Marine discharged before her EAS for pregnancy and any Marine separated while in a sole parent status. SRB entry required stating reason for assignment. Individual Marine must sign SRB entry. CMC authority required for reenlistment.

REENLISTMENT CODES

Code	When Assigned	Remarks
RE-30	Refused to extend or reenlist to obtain the obligated service necessary to carry out PCS or UDP.	SRB entry required stating reason for assignment. Individual Marine must sign SRB entry and have the opportunity to submit a statement. Forward signed copies of page 11 entry and statement (if any) to CMC (MMSB). Refer to MCO P1300.8. This code may only be assigned when directed by CMC and is not assigned to first-term Marines. Marines assigned this code are not eligible for promotion, reenlistment, commissioning or warrant officer programs, special education programs, or in voluntary separation pay. CMC authority required for reenlistment.
RE-3P	Failure to meet physical/medical standards (includes pseudofolliculitis and weight standards).	Recommended by CO upon removal of disqualifying factor. SRB entry required stating reason for assignment. Individual Marine must sign SRB entry. CMC authority required for reenlistment.
RE-3S	The Marine is approved for voluntary separation and receives the Special Separation Benefit (SSB), lump sum payment. May only be assigned by the CMC.	Marine is recommended and eligible for reenlistment. Assigned when Marine meets eligibility criteria established in ALMAR announcing programs. This is a voluntary separation used to effect the military drawdown. SRB entry is required stating Marine agrees to separate between the window established by ALMAR and Marine must sign a written agreement to serve in the IRR for 3 years. CMC approval required for reenlistment.

REENLISTMENT CODES

Code	When Assigned	Remarks
RE-3V	The Marine is approved for voluntary separation and receives the Voluntary Separation Incentive (VSI), annuity payment. May only be assigned by the CMC.	Same criteria established for SSB program (above) except Marine must sign agreement to serve in the IRE for the duration of the VSI payment period.
RE-4	Not recommended for reenlistment.	SRB entry required stating reason for assignment. Individual Marine must sign SRB entry. This code may be assigned in lieu of any RE-3 code (except RE-3B and RE-3F) if the Marine's performance warrants and the reason can be documented.
RE-4B	Assign when there is a military or civil record of in-service illegal drug involvement and there is no potential for further service.	SRB entry required stating reason for assignment. Individual Marine must sign SRB entry.

I-4

Oath of Office

Oath of Enlistment/Reenlistment

Oath of Office

"I DO SOLEMNLY SWEAR (OR AFFIRM) THAT I WILL SUPPORT AND DEFEND THE CONSTITUTION OF THE UNITED STATES AGAINST ALL ENEMIES, FOREIGN AND DOMESTIC; THAT I WILL BEAR TRUE FAITH AND ALLEGIANCE TO THE SAME; THAT I TAKE THIS OBLIGATION FREELY; WITHOUT ANY MENTAL RESERVATION OR PURPOSE OF EVASION; AND THAT I WILL WELL AND FAITHFULLY DISCHARGE THE DUTIES OF THE OFFICE ON WHICH I AM ABOUT TO ENTER; SO HELP ME GOD."

Oath of Enlistment/Reenlistment

"I (STATE YOUR NAME) DO SOLEMNLY SWEAR (OR AFFIRM) THAT I WILL SUPPORT AND DEFEND THE CONSTITUTION OF THE UNITED STATES AGAINST ALL ENEMIES, FOREIGN AND DOMESTIC; THAT I WILL BEAR TRUE FAITH AND ALLEGIANCE TO THE SAME; AND THAT I WILL OBEY THE ORDERS OF THE PRESIDENT OF THE UNITED STATES AND THE ORDERS OF THE OFFICERS APPOINTED OVER ME, ACCORDING TO THE REGULATIONS AND THE UNIFORM CODE OF MILITARY JUSTICE. SO HELP ME GOD."

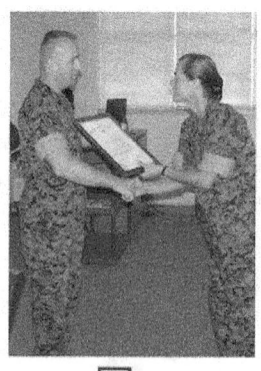

Commonly Used Admin References

Absentee/Deserter/UA:	MCO P5800.16 MCO P1070.12
Active Duty Operational Support (ADOS)	MCO 1001.59
Administrative Procedures	MCO P5000.14
Awards and Decorations	SECNAV 1650.1 MCO 1650.19
Casualty Program	MCO P3040.4
Command Issued Directives/Directives Control Point	MCO 5215.1 NAVMC 5215.1

Entitlements
  -Family Separation Allowance (FSA)
  -Basic Allowance for Subsistence (BAS)
  -Basic Allowance for Housing (BAH)
	DODFMR Vol 7A
	MCO 10110.47
	MCO P1751.3
	JFTR

Leave, Liberty, and Administrative Absence	MCO P1050.3
Military Occupational Specialty Manual	MCO P1200.7
Official Mail Program	MCO 5110.4
Personnel Orders	MCO P1000.6 MCO 1300.8 MCO P1326.6 MCO 4650.30
Performance Evaluation System	MCO P1610.7 MCO 1610.11 MCO 1610.15
Promotion/Reductions	MCO P1400.31 MCO P1400.32
Retirements/Resignations/Transfer to FMCR	MCO P1900.16 MCO P1400.31
Reserve Administration	MCO P1001R.1
Service Records	MCO P1070.12
Travel	NAVSO P-6034 (JFTR)
Unit Diary	MCTFSPRIUM MCO P1080.20
Unit Punishment Book/Legal Issues	MCO P5800.16 MCM 2008 JAG Manual
Request Mast	MCO 1700.23

Commonly Used Phone Numbers

Manpower Management (MM)	703-784-xxxx DSN 278-xxxx
Evaluation Review	9205
Enlisted Assignments	9328
Officer Assignments	9284
Support Branch	3934
Promotion Branch	
-Enlisted	9710
-Officer	9703
Separation & Retirements	9304
Military Awards	9206
Casualty Branch	9580
Reserve Affairs (RA)	
Manpower	9104
Career Management Team	9127
Marine For Life Program	9104
MCCAT East	910-450-1251 DSN 750
Fax	0981
MCCAT West	760-725-3085 DSN 361
Fax	760-725-3117
MISSO-02 (Camp Lejeune)	910-450-2708 DSN 750
MISSO-03 (Camp Pendleton)	760-725-6982 DSN 365
MISSO-06 (Hawaii)	808-257-1334 DSN 457
MISSO-09 (District of Columbia)	703-784-9054 DSN 278
MISSO-16/17 (Kansas City)	816-926-5188 DSN 465
MISSO-27 (Okinawa, Japan)	DSN 6452966/3415
DFAS Kansas City	800-594-8302
MyPay	800-390-2348 DSN 580-5122
Thrift Savings Plan	877-968-3778
PA School (Admin Support)	910-450-0933
PA School (Entry Level)	910-450-1073
PA School (Career Level)	910-450-1791

Commonly Used Admin Links/Websites

Awards
https://lnweb1.manpower.usmc.mil/manpower/mm/mmma/awardsref.nsf

Active Duty Retirement System
http://www.dod.mil/militarypay/retirement/ad/index.html

ACE Military Guides
http://www.militaryguides.acenet.edu/

ALMARS
http://www.marines.mil/news/messages/Pages/almars

BAH Rate Inquiry
http://www.dtic.mil/perdiem/bahform.html

Defense Link
http://www.defenselink.mil

DEERS Address Change
https://www.dmdc.osd.mil/appj/address/index.jsp

DOD Travel Regs
http://www.dtic.mil/perdiem/trvlregs.html

DOD Directives
http://www.dtic.mil/whs/directives

DOD Forms
http://www.dtic.mil/whs/directives/infomgt/forms/formsprogram.htm

DODFMR
http://www.dod.mil/comptroller/fmr/

Defense Travel System
http://www.defensetravel.osd.mil/dts/site/index.jsp

DTS Travel Center
http://www.dtstravelcenter.dod.mil/Index.cfm

Enlisted Assignments
https://lnweb1.manpower.usmc.mil/manpower/mi/mra_ofct.nsf/MMEA/Enlisted%20Ass

ignments%20Branch%20Home

Enlisted Promotions
https://lnweb1.manpower.usmc.mil/manpower/mi/mra_ofct.nsf/MMPR/Enlisted+Promo
tion+Home

Federal Voting Assistance Program
http://www.fvap.gov

Foreign PerDiem Rates
http://www.state.gov/m/a/als/prdm/
JAG Manual
http://neds.nebt.daps.mil/jag/jag.htm

JFTR
http://141.116.74.201/cgi-bin/om_isapi.dll?clientID=101132&infobase=jftr.nfo&softpage=Browse_Frame_Pg42

Marine Online
https://www.mol.usmc.mil/System/TFAS/Login.asp

Marine Corps Home Page
http://www.usmc.mil

Marine For Life Program
https://www.m4l.usmc.mil/portal/server.pt

Marine Corps Publications
http://www.usmc.mil/directiv.nsf/web+orders

Marine Corps Service Support Schools
http://www.lejeune.usmc.mil/mccsss/

Marine Net
https://www.marinenet.usmc.mil/portal/

MMSB Home Page
https://www.mmsb.usmc.mil

MARADMINS
http://www.marines.mil/maradmins/maradmin2000.nsf/maradmins

MCCAT East
http://www.lejeune.usmc.mil/mcaat/

Manpower & Reserve Affairs (M&RA)
https://lnweb1.manpower.usmc.mil/manpower/mi/mra_ofct.nsf/m&ra+home

Military Pay and Benefits
http://www.dod.mil/militarypay/

MISSA/MISSO Portal
http://www.missa.manpower.usmc.mil/

MCI
https://www.mci.usmc.mil/newmci

MGIB
http://www.gibill.va.gov/

My Pay
https://mypay.dfas.mil/mypay.aspx

National Records Center
http://www.archives.gov
Officer Assignments
https://lnweb1.manpower.usmc.mil/manpower/mi/mra_ofct.nsf/MMOA/Officer+Assignments+Branch+Home

Officer Promotions

https://lnweb1.manpower.usmc.mil/manpower/mi/mra_ofct.nsf/MMPR/Officer+Promotion+Home

Personnel Administration Home Page
http://www.lejeune.usmc.mil/mccsss/schools/pas/pas.shtml

Per Diem Rates
http://www.dtic.mil/perdiem/perdiemrates.html

Pay Charts
http://www.dfas.mil/money/milpay/index.htm

Personnel Admin Advisory (PAA)
https://lnweb1.manpower.usmc.mil/manpower/mi/mra_ofct.nsf/mif/Personnel+Admin+Advisory+Messages(PAA)

POV Mileages Rates
http://www.dtic.mil/perdiem/faqmilea.html

Online PRIUM
http://www.missa.manpower.usmc.mil/default.asp?id=90&mnu=90

Overseas COLA Query
http://www.dtic.mil/perdiem/ocform.html

Online Code Manual
http://www.missa.manpower.usmc.mil/default.asp?id=92&mnu=92

Retirement Calculators
http://www.defenselink.mil/militarypay/retirement/calc/index.html

Selective Service Registration
https://www4.sss.gov/regver/register1.asp

Separations Home Page
https://lnweb1.manpower.usmc.mil/manpower/mi/mra_ofct.nsf/MMSR/Separation+and+Retirement+Branch+Home

SMART Transcripts
https://smart.cnet.navy.mil/

Staff Judge Advocate
http://sja.hqmc.usmc.mil

Training and Education Command
http://www.tecom.usmc.mil/

Table of Official Distances
http://dtod.sddc.army.mil/
Thrift Savings Plan
http://www.tsp.gov

Veterans Affairs
http://www.va.gov

Verification of Military Education
https://www.dmdc.osd.mil/vmet/owa/vmet_web_display.login